APR 13 1999

VOCATIONAL GUIDANCE

WITHDRAWN

Household Careers:
Nannies, Butlers, Maids & More

The Complete Guide for Finding
Household Employment
or
"If the dog likes you, you're hired!"

Copyright © 1993, by Linda F. Radke, Scottsdale, AZ

The pages marked SAMPLE(s) may be duplicated at will. Otherwise, all rights reserved. No part of this book may be reproduced, stored in a retrieval system or transcribed in any means, electronic, mechanical, photocopying, recording or otherwise, without the written permission of the publisher. For information, write to: Five Star Publications, P.O. Box 3142-FSP, Scottsdale, AZ 85271-3142, Scottsdale, AZ 85271-3142, (602) 941-0770.

"This publication is designed to provide accurate and authoritative information in regard to the subject matter covered. It is sold with the understanding that the publisher and author are not engaged in rendering legal, accounting, or other professional service."

From a Declaration jointly adopted by a Committee of the American Bar Association and a Committee of Publishers.

ISBN: 1-877749-05-2
Library of Congress Catalog Number:

Library of Congress Cataloging in Publication Data:

Radke, Linda F.
Household careers: nannies, butlers, maids and more: the complete guide for finding household employment, or "–if the dog likes you, you're hired!" / Linda F. Radke
    p. cm.
Includes bibliographical references and index.
ISBN 1-877749-05-2: $14.95
1. Domestics. 2. Job hunting. I. Title.
HD8039. D5833 1993   93-19218
640'.23'73--dc20   CIP

Edited by Mary E. Hawkins
Text illustrated by Lynlie Hermann
Cover design by Christine Barringer and Terri Macdonald
Book design and production by Two Macs Type & Design

Printed in the United States of America

Household Careers:
Nannies, Butlers, Maids & More

The Complete Guide for Finding
Household Employment

or

"If the dog likes you, you're hired!"

Linda F. Radke

The Household Workers'
Bill of Rights

A household worker has a right...

to be called a nanny or butler upon receiving proper training

to a job description

to be hired to care for a child and nothing but the child

to work 40 hours per week with two days off per week

to designated hours "off"

to a competitive salary

to be or not to be a part of a family

to safe working conditions

to feedback on job performance

to references when leaving

to be assured that employment meets all legal and tax requirements.

DEDICATED TO THE MEMORY OF

UNCLE SEYMOUR

A NOTE FROM THE AUTHOR

This book was written to be an informative book on finding household employment. The idea is to present information that will open your employment opportunities. Names of certain schools, associations, and agencies are mentioned throughout the book. The listings are given as a source of information. The listing is not given as an endorsement, recommendation, or a referral. I strongly suggest and encourage you to check references of any service, school, or association before entering into a formal agreement. If you select a school, ask about placement opportunities. Ask for statistics on past placements. Ask for references. It is always a good idea to check with the Better Business Bureau in the state in which the business operates.

I devoted a special chapter to butlers. So many think of the butler as a thing of the past, a dying profession. It is alive and well. I felt it deserved a chapter of its own.

In *Household Careers* I have tried to avoid the awkward "him or her" form to indicate that the statement applies to either men or women. In its place, I have used the plural form, or the gender most usually associated with the position under discussion. This is not to mean that either sex is excluded from any job category.

Special Thanks To...

Each person that helped with this book gave more than their time... they gave their excellence... they went beyond the pages... they helped give this book life... they have been an incredible team to work with... thank each of you for going beyond the call of duty...

For the reviewers who took time from their busy schedules to review Household Careers... thank you... having Julie Berkel review this book was a little like being back in English 101... thank you for not using a red pen and for your kindness... I hope your students appreciate you as much as they should – now... English 101.... one never really understands just how important that class is...

My editor, Mary E. Hawkins, who helped turn my thoughts into words — words into chapters — and chapters into a book.

My graphic designer, Terri Macdonald — whose talents go far beyond designing. Thanks for all your hard work and input. Your work made all the difference.

Lynlie Hermann, who did an incredible job illustrating this book. Good work!

Michelle — Thank you for taking such good care of Gradey. For the endless trips to the park and to the zoo and for all the thoughtful things you do. Thank you.

TOP 10 REASONS FOR DOING HOUSEHOLD WORK

1. Sure beats working for food
2. Expensive dirt feels good
3. Expensive dirt feels good
4. Adds to my total perception of what life is all about
5. Adds to my qualifications as a spouse
6. Looks good when applying for C.E.O.
7. Gives me a good reason to retire young
8. Good exercise — sure cheaper than joining a health club
9. Gives me a good excuse for not doing my own cleaning
10. Keeps me in touch with the IRS

Contents

Foreword xi

Prologue
Mary Poppins, where are you? 1

Getting Started
Get on your mark, get set, get ready. 5

Butlers
The butler did it and so can you... 7

Wall Street Nannies
It's a rising market. 11

Options in Household Jobs
Definitions. Who does what? 13

I Need Work
Where's that mirror? 23

Getting the Facts Together
The whole truth and nothing but the truth 27

Creative Marketing
To market... to market 33

More Ads
More on responding to ads 45

Interviewing
Can we talk? 49

Firming Up the Agreement
Signed, sealed, delivered 55

I Want This Job to Last
For better or worse, richer or poorer 61

Quitting
Take this job and... 65

Through the Looking Glass
Creating your own job 69

The Ball Is in Your Court
Take aim... 75

Samples
It's right here in black and white... 79

References
.... 91

Index
.... 99

Foreword

Every day throughout the schools of America students question their future: *Where am I going? What am I going to do with my life?* Not all students answer, "To a university and four-year degree program." Caring educators constantly offer alternatives to those students who add: *I don't know. What can I do?* These educational advisors suggest that students take career skills and interest surveys, that they build on the skills and interests they already have, that they research career materials to find options that suit their skills and interests.

Linda F. Radke's **HOUSEHOLD CAREERS: Nannies, Butlers, Maids & More – The Complete Guide for Finding Household Employment** or *"If the dog likes you, you're hired!"* offers a clearly understandable, direct answer for the household career field. This highly informative resource book provides a wealth of information to career educators, guidance counselors, work experience advisors, home economics or life management teachers, and other educators who guide students in their career

Household Careers: Nannies, Butler, Maids & More

explorations. Covering the fields of household management and child care, the handbook defines 25 job titles; gives advice on writing resumés and cover letters; presents samples; and offers clues to the hiring perspective of employers.

HOUSEHOLD CAREERS is an excellent primary source for students who want to know what household careers are available, what pay ranges exist, and how to seek and land these jobs. Students can easily propel themselves into a career by following Radke's advice. Libraries, career centers, guidance offices, and home economics/life management offices would service students well by carrying copies of this book because of its up-to-date information, readability, and practicality.

Julianne M. Berkel
English Department Chairperson
Saguaro High School
Scottsdale, Arizona

Prologue

Mary Poppins, where are you?

It takes more than a spoonful of sugar to help employers find household help. Employers are paying premium prices for household care. Agencies are being paid hundreds, if not thousands, of dollars to find the right person to care for homes or loved ones.

What does it take to get these jobs, find them and keep them?

My first book, ***Nannies, Maids & More: The Complete Guide for Hiring Household Help***, is helping thousands of families find household workers. It gives clues on how to find, screen, and keep household employees.

This book addresses the other side of that coin: the household worker. How do you go about finding the best paying jobs? How do you catch the big ones? That is the subject of this book.

From 1983-1988, I operated a household employment agency in Scottsdale, Arizona. During that time, I helped more than 1,000 families find household help. Through the process, more than 5,000 applicants were screened. ***Nannies, Maids & More*** was written with the employer's point of view in mind. It tells how to find and keep household help and how to avoid the common pitfalls when hiring household help.

A lot has happened since ***Nannies, Maids & More***. I sold my agency, continued publishing, started consulting, writing, and adopted a baby. Now I am writing again.

My first publication, in 1985, was ***The Domestic Screening Kit***. It was a kit composed of advice for the individual looking to hire any type of household help. It had actual forms that could be used for screening and interviewing household help. The kit achieved local notoriety. Nearly every paper in town wrote about the kit and my agency.

The media questioned why I would offer the advice

in a kit and still expect clients to hire my service to find them a household employee. The truth is, the process is tedious, cumbersome, and filled with liabilities. The kit soon taught that the roads were long, the process time-consuming, and no matter who did the job, it was not easy. Finding qualified people is a challenge, keeping them even greater. So the kit was my first experience with publishing. The urge to publish only grew greater.

I then created *Options: A Directory of Child and Senior Services*. It was an Arizona-based directory that offered information about the various forms of help. It listed day care centers, child care for sick children, sitting services, nanny agencies, senior care services, adult day care, nursing homes, and the like. It showed the options for people in need of help. This second publication further implanted the seed to continue publishing. I knew I was hooked.

My husband and I discussed my options. We knew that we were longing to adopt a child. We knew that once we had a baby, I would want to be home. I also knew that running a business from an outside office would limit my time at home with our future child. We decided that if I could sell my agency, I would do so. It would allow me to have an office at my home, be closer to our child, and continue publishing. The rest is history. In 1988 I sold my agency. The people who bought my agency have nourished it, as I did, and they have a better than ever business, still flourishing.

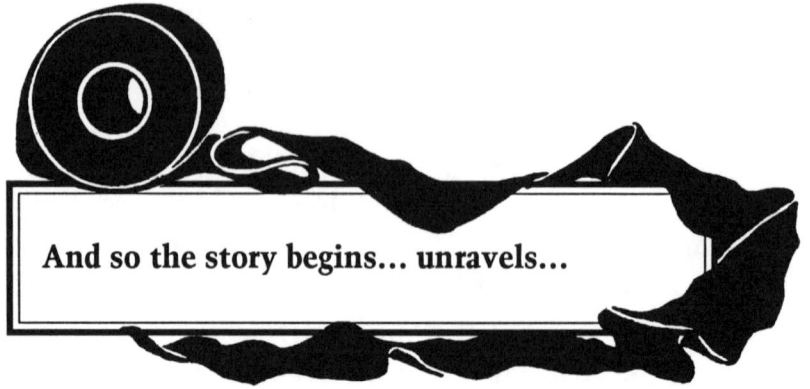

And so the story begins... unravels...

Getting Started

*Get on your mark,
get set, get ready.*

    This book is *the* map to household employment. It explains how to find the better paying jobs, how to get hired, how to stay employed. It will help you understand the real value of the jobs and why they deserve greater respect than they sometimes get. The value that you place on yourself, how professional you are, adds to the value that others put on your work. The more professional you are, the higher salary and respect the job merits, and the more likely you are to get the better jobs.

    The suggestions in this book will help you build that professionalism and give you the edge needed to gain the best jobs in money and satisfaction. They will show you how to analyze and market your skills.

After reading this book, you will have learned about:

- the definitions of 25 different household jobs
  (or know the difference from one household job to another... for example, what a mother's helper does, versus a nanny)
- skills needed for each job title
- how to find the better paying jobs
- how to better market yourself
- how to prepare your resumé *(samples provided)*
- how to have your references available
- how to close an agreement
- the IRS's and other legal requirements
- which courses to take to upgrade your chances
- how to hold your job
- how to leave your job.

Remember, even though you are in demand, you are not irreplaceable. It may take time for your employer to replace you, but don't kid yourself; if you screw up your job, you are at risk of losing it.

We'll even show you how to leave a job gracefully without losing those very important references.

Now open this map and get started.

Butlers

The butler did it and so can you . . .

Butlers are alive and well and earning... well, enough to raise cheers from the IRS. Ivor Spencer, who founded the Ivor Spencer International School for Butler Administrators/Personal Assistants (taught British style) trains butlers in the United Kingdom and the United States. He has "exported" his butlers all over the world—to the United States, Germany, Switzerland, France, Italy, Saudi Arabia, and Hong Kong. He personally escorts the candidate to the prospective employer.

Spencer, employer, and butler candidate spend a day or two, usually in a smart hotel suite, going through the daily routine, helping employer and butler get to know each other. Employers, too, need some training in the relationship.

Spencer's placement agency suggests that butlers start at $35,000 plus free accommodations, food, medical care, and use of a car for shopping, plus maid service. Housemen start at around $20,000 with the same "perks."

Butlers go through an intensive six-week training that includes field trips to lunch at Claridge's, tea at the Savoy Hotel, and practice in the refinements of elegant households. These days, butlers may have to be bodyguards as well. "The rich are increasingly worried about security and sometimes want bodyguard butlers," says Spencer. Hence some butlers receive training in handling small arms, in martial arts, and in evasive driving. In America, these butlers may be paid as much as $60,000 per year.

Today's duties for butlers may also include organizing schedules and foreign travels for their employers. Some even learn to fly helicopters. One butler administrator pilots a jet for his boss in the U.S.A.

Traditionally, Spencer trains his butlers to control and run large busy households for heads of companies, royalty, and embassies. Ages may vary from 17 to 60 years, with many butlers spending most of their life with the same family. A butler's day may begin with a wake-up call to his master and then seeing to the master's breakfast and his clothes for the day. For the rest of the day, the butler orders supplies, chooses menus for dinner or parties, does the shopping, hires other household personnel, supervises the cleaning of the entire household, as well as runs large parties and provides whatever assistance is needed for the evening.

Some of the less exciting rules of training regard meticulous care of personal appearance to the extent of two baths a day, teeth cleaning at four-hour intervals, and no curry, onion, or garlic, even on days off. Butlers must be people of discretion, loyalty, and the highest integrity. They must be able to get along with everybody and act in a low-keyed manner. They must possess infinite tact, skill in all situations, and an understanding of the refinements of living, whatever the employer's locale.

Some butlers find their "niche" in luxury hotels where they become "maitres d'etages," for example, and may have other butlers, as many as 35, on their staff.

In the United States and the United Kingdom, Spencer has a school and agency for butler administrators/personal assistants; a school for bodyguard butlers; a school for housemen; and a newly opened school for nannies. In San Francisco, his U.S. courses for butlers last three weeks, but the syllabus and diploma are the same as in the U.K. In order to do the usual six-weeks course in three weeks, the students work very hard, but the course is fascinating and intensive. Spencer teaches personally in the United States. The nanny course lasts seven days; the housemen's school, seven days; and the bodyguard butler school, seven weeks, which includes the normal butler training. After passing the course as a bodyguard butler, the butler must keep up the standard with continuous training.

Household Careers: Nannies, Butler, Maids & More

For information about any of these courses or schools or the schools in the United Kingdom, inquire at the address given in the **Useful Addresses** section on page 91.

Wall Street Nannies

It's a rising market.

Have you noticed that almost any household worker is in demand? Housekeepers, nannies, senior care givers, preschool workers, and maids are valuable commodities. If traded on Wall Street, their value would only continue to soar.

The demand will continue to grow as households are run either by both working parents or by single parents supporting their families. Child care particularly is an expanding field, but for decades all household help is expected to be short of workers—and that means better pay, better working conditions, and better job selection.

For jobs in most fields, there are often 300 or more contenders fighting for the opportunity of employment. Try to get a job teaching at a community college; get in line with 300 other candidates. Try to get a job as a nanny, and the *employer* needs to get in line. That's right. You read correctly.

For every person looking for a nanny job, there are probably hundreds of employers looking to hire you. If household employers do not treat their help with care, they are at great risk of losing them.

Options in Household Jobs

Definitions. Who does what?

Household employment falls into several broad categories: child care, elder care, housekeeping, outside household work, supplementary activities. There are many jobs within each category. Choice may require flexibility on your part as well as an understanding of the duties required, the outlook for each job, prevailing salary ranges, and so on.

Definitions and specific duties may vary by locale. The following definitions are those most in use and most readily understood. A more detailed listing of duties for each can be found in the ***Dictionary of Occupational Titles*** by the U.S. Department of Labor, listed in the

References section (page 96) and in other sources also given there and generally available in libraries.

CHILD CARE

Baby Sitter Supervises activities of a child in child's own home or in motel or resorts.

Nanny In-house professional child care. Has training in child care. Ideal is full-time, long term association with the child.

A traveling nanny may travel with the family and care for the child or children.

Governess Educationally qualified person to teach school-age children in their own homes.

Mother's Helper
Provides both child care and light household tasks in home where one parent is home some or most of the time.

Family Home Day Care Provider
Provides child care in her own home for full- or part-time days or nights. (However, it is generally done during the day.) May care for several children. Licensing may be required by the state. (See Chapter 9.)

Preschool Worker
 Cares for or supervises children or directs activities in an organizational setting, such as a child care center, preschool center, church-sponsored center, employer's facility for children of employees, Head Start, or other program.

ELDER CARE

Companion For elderly, handicapped, or convalescent person. Attends to employer's personal needs, social or business affairs, reads aloud, plays games to entertain employer. Accompanies employer on trips or outings. May prepare and serve meals.

Respite Care
 Relieves the usual caregiver of an elderly or handicapped person. Usually a part-time position. Person cared for likely to be unable to get around or go out much.

HOUSEKEEPING

Head Housekeeper
 Supervises activities of household employees in a private residence employing a large staff.

Housekeeper, Maid, or General House Worker

Performs duties to keep private home clean and orderly. Duties generally lean toward house cleaning, but may include personal services and supervision of children. May be full-time or part-time.

Executive Housekeeper in Hotel or Resort or Group Living

Manages the housekeeping activities. Hires, trains, supervises cleaning and supply staff for rooms.

Room or Turndown Attendant

In hotel or resort. Room attendant cleans guest rooms "to the hotel's standards." Works mornings. Turndown attendant checks guest rooms in evening. Tidies room, turns down beds. Works evenings.

OTHER HOUSEHOLD

Butler — Supervises and coordinates activities of household employees. Answers telephone, receives and announces guests. Performs other services as requested. (May have special training in butler's school. See page 8.)

Cook Prepares meals. May plan meals and/or do shopping. Cleans kitchen.

Launderer Washes, irons, or presses family clothes and household linens. May work in family residence or in own home.

Driver or Chauffeur Drives family members wherever they wish to go. Maintains, cares for vehicles. Runs errands.

OUTSIDE HOUSEHOLD WORK

Yard Worker Keeps grounds of private residence in neat and orderly condition. May also work for apartment complex, hotel, other multi-residence installation.

Gardener Plants and cares for flower beds, lawns, other plantings at single or multiple residences. May plan the plantings.

Caretaker Looks after private property. May be left in charge during owner's absence.

SUPPLEMENTARY HELP

Pet Sitter — Looks after pets during owners' absence.

House Sitter — Stays in and looks after a house during owners' absence.

Elderly Sitter — Caregiver for elderly person in home or in motels and resorts.

Sitters — Sitters can be hired to care for children, elderly, pets, or homes.

Caterer — Provides special foods or entire meals on an as-ordered basis. May provide china, table linens, chairs for large events.

Party Server — Engaged to come in and help serve a large or special affair. May work cooperatively with a caterer.

Live-in or Live-out Couples — A couple (often married) working cooperatively in almost any combination of above jobs. For example, chauffeur-housekeeper; caretaker-elder companion; groundskeeper-cook.

Obviously, in most of these positions, you may work either independently or as part of a team or contracting service which seeks out the jobs and is, in effect, your employer.

As mentioned before, for more detailed descriptions of duties and alternate titles, see the government's *Dictionary of Occupational Titles*, *The Occupational Outlook Handbook*, and *Occupational Careers Sourcebook*. All are listed in the **References** on pages 96 and 97.

The following chart shows general categories of employment and comparative rates of pay.

Survey of Household Help Salary Ranges*

In dollars per week unless otherwise noted.

Position	City	Live In	Live Out	Part Time
Nanny	Anchorage	200-300	250-350	5-7/hr.
	Boston	250-350	275-450	9-12/hr.
	Chicago	250-300	250-325	5-7/hr.
	Cleveland	200-350	300-350	6-7/hr.
	Columbia, MD	200-250	200-300	5-8/hr.
	Dallas	350-500	350-500	6.50-10/hr.
	Ft. Lauderdale	175-400	175-400	
	New York	250-400	300-550	7-10/hr.
	Phoenix	225-350	225-350	
	Seattle	250-375	250-300	7-10/hr.
	Tampa**	180-325	250-375	6-10/hr.
Baby Nurse	Seattle			8-10/hr.
	Tampa**	525-700	450-700	6.50-10/hr.
			65-100/day	
Governess	Phoenix	20,000-30,000/yr.		
	Seattle		1,500-2,000/mth.	
Elder or Senior Care				
	Anchorage			7-9/hr.
	Boston	400-1200/mth.		
	Dallas	300-350	300-350	10/hr. (ill senior care)
	Phoenix	300	300	60-90/day
	Seattle	300-425	300-375	8-10/hr.
	Tampa**	200-300	250-350	5-8/hr.
Housekeeper				
	Anchorage			9/hr.
	Boston	350-600	12-20/hr.	12-20/hr.
	Dallas	400-600	400-600	
	Ft. Lauderdale	175-400	175-400	
	Phoenix	250-450	8-15/hr.	
	Seattle		10-12/hr.	
	Tampa**			7-10/hr.

Position	City	Live In	Live Out	Part Time
Baby Sitter	Anchorage			5-6/hr.
	Boston	150-250	225-300	6-10/hr.
	Dallas	275-325	275-325	
	Phoenix	225-350	225-350	
	Seattle		6-7/hr.	
	Tampa**	60-100/day Temp.		5-8/hr.
Butler	Boston	450-1200	450-1200	
	Phoenix			12-15/hr.
	Seattle	375-500	300-450	10-12/hr.
Butler Administrator				
	Dallas	2,500-6,000/mth.		
Butler Bodyguard		Up to 60,000/yr.		
Chauffer	Dallas	2,500/mth.	2,500/mth.	
	Phoenix			15/hr.
	Seattle		1,200/mth.	
Cook/Chef	Boston	10-15/hr.		
	Dallas	625-875	625-875	
	Phoenix	10-15/hr.		
	Seattle		15-20/hr.	
	Tampa**			9-10/hr.
Couple	Boston	300-1,000		
	Dallas	4,000-8,000 per month on a yearly basis		
	Phoenix	18,000-36,000/yr.		
	Seattle		1,200-2,000	
Butler/Cook	Dallas	625-1500		
Gardener	Dallas	500-625	500-625	

* The salary ranges given here represent general ranges supplied by agencies placing household workers. Salary ranges will vary from one agency to another and one city to another. All of the agencies that responded to my questionnaire are well established and have been in business for at least three years. Please note that most of the better paying household jobs are offered through agencies. The typical classified ad placed by an individual will most likely not pay as well.

** The figures supplied for Tampa include St. Petersburg, Clearwater, and Sarasota as well as the Florida counties of Hillsborough, Pinellas, Pasco, Sarasota, and Manatee.

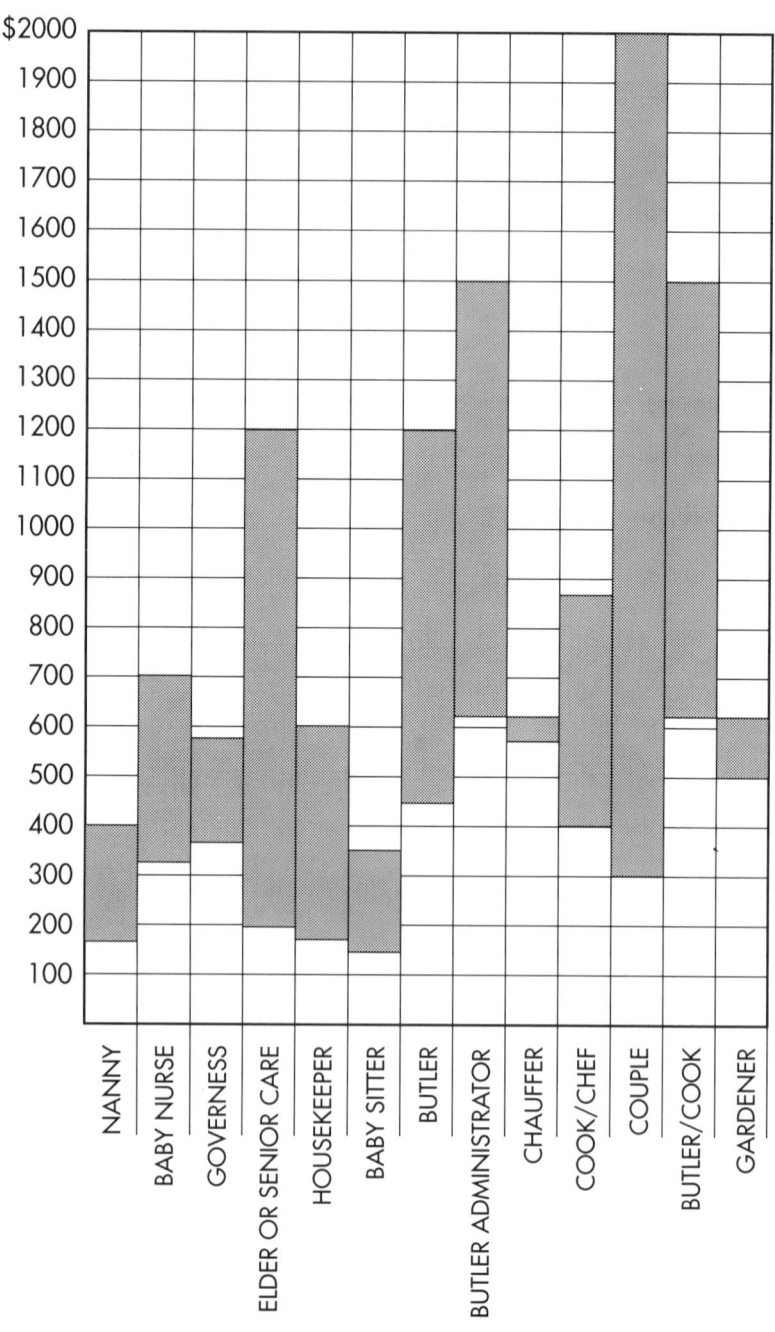

I Need Work

Where's that mirror?

We've already laid out the bare bones of 25 jobs that are in demand in almost every location. Look at each job individually. Do you like child care or supervision, or would you prefer the quiet adult conversation of an older person? Or do you like working with household furnishings and activities, or want to work out of doors? Already you're part way there!

Now rough out your needs and skills and begin to match them to the jobs in the area you are looking into.

"Mirror, mirror on the wall . . . tell me true, what, oh what, shall I do?"

What is my training, background?

What are my financial needs? Hopes?

What is my time frame? Do I need a job right away or can I look around a bit, even get more preparation?

What do I have now and what can I acquire with the time, money, and skills I have?

Here's an example: If you are looking into child care, you need to consider the following when looking for work:

If you like the idea of working with children, but not around the parent or parents, you wouldn't want to apply for a mother's helper position. Generally speaking, a mother's helper assists in the care of the children while the mother is in the home, at least most of the time. I personally have a mother's helper working for me. It offers me the best of both worlds. As I write this book, Michelle is caring for Gradey. He is just a little under two years old now. I'm not ready to have him in a day care center. (I don't know if I'll ever be ready for that.) I want to be able to work from my home, yet still be close to my son. This allows me to get my work done, run errands, and take some time away from my son — time away that we both need.

I Need Work

When I pre-screened callers, I first asked if they were comfortable working in a home where the mother would be working out of the home office. I would say that 90 percent felt comfortable with the idea, about 10 percent were adamantly against the idea. With those, I spared both of us the interview.

What other options are open to you in child care? You can work in a public day care center, church or synagogue day care center, or be a teacher's aide. Day care centers generally pay minimum wage (now $4.25/hr.). Most in-home workers that are placed through an agency in the Phoenix area can expect to earn $4-$6 per hour when doing in-home, live-out, child care.

The benefit to being a teacher's aide is that you can expect a slightly higher income and benefits. (I hope our mother's helper doesn't get hold of this chapter.) Moreover, both as a teacher's aide and as a staff member of a good day care center, you will build up your own knowledge of child development and training techniques.

You need to consider your emotional needs. Do you need a room filled with active people, or does that sound too stressful? If so, then home employment is for you.

Here's another possibility if you have office skills. You can consider working for an agency that places household helpers. There are such agencies throughout the country. Look in the Yellow Pages under Sitting Services, Nanny Agencies, Day Care, Child Care, and the like.

What have you learned about yourself? Develop a list of your likes and dislikes.

LIKES	*DISLIKES*
Caring for newborns	*Doing dishes*
Doing laundry	*Driving*
Keeping a house tidy	*Washing windows*
Taking walks	*Helping with homework*
Baking cookies	
Reading to someone	

If you still aren't quite certain about the best place for you, many universities, community colleges, and high schools offer career counseling.

You can find good testing grounds in temporary services such as:

- Caring for children
- Nursing companion
- Housecleaning on a temporary basis.

Try to find the job that best suits your likes. No job is going to be perfect.

Getting the Facts Together

The whole truth and nothing but the truth

Once you see a good match between possible jobs and your qualifications and interests, the next step is to get the facts together. However you go about getting the job, you will need a good resumé, a set of facts about your work experience and qualifications.

Organize your past and target your future.

Having all this down in black and white will help you be specific, whether you are discussing the job over the phone, preparing for an interview, or planning your employment strategy.

A resumé should identify the position you are interested in, but most employers aren't interested in long flowery statements of your ultimate goals. If you are considering two jobs in different areas, make a resumé for each. For more help on resumés, check the books in your library. There are many good instruction manuals. Samples are given in the **References** section.

For every resumé, include:

- *Name, address, phone number, Social Security No.*
- *Position sought*
- *Experience*

    Leave no gaps in time.

    List in reverse order, beginning with most recent.

    Include name of employer and of supervisor with address and telephone number.

    Give a brief description of duties performed or job title.

- *Education*

    Include formal education and any special courses applicable to the position sought.

    Include names of schools, locations, dates attended, degree or certificate earned.

    List more recent first. (Older workers can cut down on this section in favor of more space for experience.)

- *References*

    Include some references from your work situations, some as character references.

    You may also indicate "Available on request."

A special word here about references. One general area of weakness I detected in most candidates applying for household help was references. Most people leave one job without thought of obtaining a reference. If you or your employer will be leaving the area or if the employer will not be available for inquiries, ask for a "To Whom It May Concern" statement that you can use as a reference. If you come prepared with written references, an agency or future employer can always call your references if they have additional questions. Coming prepared with these reference forms completed will look highly professional.

- *Organizations, hobbies, and personal interests*

    This is an optional section of a resumé. It can help

build up your personality and suggest areas of compatibility, especially for child care or senior care positions. For example: sports, or work as a volunteer in a reading for the blind program. If you are looking for a step ahead as a gardener or groundskeeper, mention any garden or environmental groups you belong to and any awards you and/or the homeowner have won for flowers or landscaping.

- *Length*

    Try to hold your resumé to one, or at most two, pages.

- *Make it look nice.*

With word processors and computers as well as typewriters so readily available today, it is easy to prepare a neat page. In fact, there is no excuse not to. Even if you have to have one of the duplicating services set it up for you, the expense may be worth it, and copies can be run off for very few cents each.

The Cover Letter

(See the **Samples** section beginning on page 79.)

If you are submitting your resumé "cold" or in answer to a help wanted ad, keep the letter brief. Simply state why you are submitting the resumé.

For example: *"In response to your advertisement in the Anytown Gazette of June 5, ..."* This identification

Getting the Facts Together

---

of date is important for the recipient, but also for you. Always keep a copy of the cover letter. If you have a form letter that you send to several addresses, just note on the letter, "Also sent to..." or "Same letter sent to..." with the date for each. You'll be surprised how easy it is to forget where you have already made contacts. Start a folder marked "Job Search" for copies of letters and resumés.

Address the letter to a name if possible. You can always call the organization and ask for a name, perhaps through the Human Resources Department. Or ask for the name of the director of a child care service or the like.

Get All Your Ducks In A Row!

Creative Marketing

To market . . . to market

All right—I've got a good product—*ME*—now, who'll buy?

Every good product needs good packaging—honest, attractive, attention-getting packaging. Without that, even the best product sits on a shelf, or waits at an empty mailbox or silent telephone.

Your own attitude, appearance, and expectations are part of this packaging. Put yourself in the place of your prospective employer.

Equally important will be your resumé or written presentation if your first contact will be by mail or an agency appointment. Follow the guidelines in the last chapter.

All right, you have three essentials:
- Your target goal—the job you want.
- Your self-confidence that this job will be right for you.
- Appealing packaging and presentation.

What next? MARKET RESEARCH. What and where is the market for the product?

If you are interested in being a housekeeper, you know right off that you will want to locate in a middle class, professional, or affluent neighborhood. If you want to be a mother's helper, you'll look for an area of young families, probably upward-bound young professionals, either working at home or with obligations or social duties outside the home. If you want to be a butler or chauffeur, you're definitely looking at affluent areas and probably people with considerable social obligations. If you want to set up child care in your own home, you will need to be within transportation of areas of working parents.

You get the idea. Analyze the demand. Go where the need is.

Most of these people need you, but they have lots to lose, too. They need to know that you are trustworthy. The best paying jobs will probably be in the more affluent areas. These people need to know that you are trustworthy, but training, skill, and personality will count, too.

Remember that there are a lot of people in many neighborhoods willing to devote some discretionary income to your salary. The retired couple on a modest income may choose some household help rather than some other luxury or entertainment. The young family may be juggling its budget for some assistance with child care and may be doubly appreciative to you for making its choice a gratifying one.

By this time you probably have settled on your prime market. Now, how to reach those potential employers.

Try these:

First of all, networking and word of mouth. Ask friends who may be doing similar work if they can recommend work for you. Satisfied employers usually ask for names of possible helpers. From these friends, get such facts as: pay rates in the area; usual conditions of employment, such as fringe benefits; transportation pay; lunch; etc.

How do I go about finding the best paying jobs?

Use a professional.

Not just because I am a former owner of a household employment agency, but for the following reasons I recommend using a household employment agency.

If you are using a reputable agency, the employer will have a greater sense of security if you are screened and recommended through an agency and you might have a better sense of security about who you might be working for. Ask the agency personnel if they screen their clients. If so, if hired, do you have access to such information? I have heard nightmare stories about nannies applying for jobs and employers having less than honorable intentions. Some things are beyond agencies' screening capabilities and yours. Don't assume that just because a family has children, that makes them honorable. I was fortunate when I had my agency. I never experienced some of the frightening tales told. I don't mean to scare you, but only to remind you to use caution in this as in all other dealings with persons you don't yet know.

Reasons to use an agency

Many people who are offering the better paying positions are more likely to use an agency. Many people do not want to give out their addresses to anyone unscreened. They count on the agency to screen and then refer for interviews.

Establish a good rapport with an agency in town. If there are several agencies, you can research each one. Contact the local Better Business Bureau. See if the agency holds any unresolved complaints.

From the agency, ask up front if they charge a fee to the worker. Find out, too, what you need to bring in during your initial agency interview. This may be more than is in your resumé. I always asked each applicant to bring in the name, address, and phone number of three employers and three non-related references.

Creative Marketing

My basic pre-screening asked if the candidate had work-related experience, references, reliable transportation, a home phone, and if looking for a long term position, the willingness to make a one-year commitment. Come prepared. The agency will love you and you will have a much better chance at gaining employment.

Agency pet peeves

Of these I can speak from personal experience. I found that if candidates seeking employment set up an appointment to first meet with us and didn't show the first time, most likely they would not show the second. If for some reason you cannot make your initial appointment, call ahead and reschedule. I found that people who asked for a second appointment rarely bothered to keep it.

Keep in mind, you are competing with many more people for the better paying positions. When we screened for a house manager, paying $400 per week, we had a lot of professionals from all fields applying. You first need to decide how serious you are about entering or continuing in the household field of employment. If your background reflects stability, the greater your chance of being given an opportunity to interview.

An agency will save both you and the prospective employer considerable time. Being known to a good agency is a great help in the future, too.

The **Application for Employment** form in the **Samples** at the end of the book (see page 86) is one I developed for my agency to record information about an applicant. It gives you an idea of what agencies and potential employers want to know about applicants.

FINDING JOB OPPORTUNITIES

People are out there, crying for help. Use these sources for finding out about job openings:

Newspaper classified advertising

Look for Help Wanted ads in these headings:
- Child Care
- Help Wanted
  (Domestic or Household may be mentioned.)
- Senior Care
- Home Health Care or Medical/Dental
- Community job listing services
- Department of Economic Security (or similar title in your location)
- Churches/Synagogues. Many churches and synagogues have listings on bulletin boards or in newsletters. Inquire.
- Schools, colleges, universities, and high schools often have job placement centers. Inquire.

Yellow Page listings

These are sources of jobs. Look under these headings:

- Child Care
- Child Guidance
- Information and Referral Services
- Sitting Services
- Nanny Agencies
- Maids and Butlers
- House Cleaning
- Nurses
- Nurses—Registries (These may be strictly in the health field.)
- Schools—Preschools and Kindergarten

TAKING THE INITIATIVE

Placing an ad for household work wanted

Classified advertising under a Work Wanted heading may be a very effective way of attracting potential employers. However, such ads can be costly for an unemployed person, particularly if you may be running the ad more than one time.

Study the ads in your local paper and practice saying as much as possible in few words. The paper will usually help you with abbreviations. Take care to say enough to give information and some uniqueness to your ad. Here is a random selection of terms from the Miscellaneous Services [offered] and Help Wanted ads in the Sunday edition of a paper in a large Southwestern city:

> *former kindergarten teacher*
> *companion for my 4-yr.-old son*
> *CPR, first aid certified*
> *share our nanny*
> *fenced yard*
> *experienced, with references*
> *non-smoking*
> *baby sit three nights*
> *education and crafts*
> *exch. room, board*
> *Mon to Fri*
> *must be U.S. citizen*
> *meals*
> *must like cats*
> *no pets*
> *swimmer*
> *infant, child care by registered nurse*
> *some travel*
> *bring DMV (Dep. Motor Vehicle) report*

The ads also carried the usual address or general location and telephone number as well.

Creative Marketing

When placing an ad, be specific, list job title wanted, state live in or live out, salary requirement, locations desired, state experience, and note that you have references available.

If you are advertising for child care in your home, say something about your location and if meals are provided. (In Phoenix, where a distressing number of young children drown in the prevalent home pools, many ads note "no swimming pool.")

Decide whether to give your home phone number in the ad. People would probably be more receptive to talking to you than making contact in some other way. If you don't want to give out your home address, then rent a P.O. box. Some newspapers offer the use of their P.O. box or assign a box number to your ad. Find out what the paper offers.

The same places that might post Help Wanted notices might very well also post Positions Wanted. Such contacts have the effect of a certain amount of screening of replies.

Samples of want ads

Here are a few sample ads that give basic information in a condensed want ad form.

> *Live-in couple available. Exp. & References. Non-smokers. Call 602-555-1212 or write Box 5555, Any Town, U.S.A. 55555*

Household Careers: Nannies, Butler, Maids & More

Live-in Nanny available. Exp. with toddlers. Loves to swim. Will travel. Exp. & References available. Call 602-555-1214 or write Box 5556, Any Town, U.S.A. 55555

Live-out Senior Care. Lots of exp/references and patience. Need $6/hr. Call... or write...

Fast, efficient house cleaning. Exp. Bonded. Refs. day work. Call 000-535-1111 or write P.O. Box 5557, Any Town, 55555.

Butler-Chauffeur. 10 yrs. last post. Wishes relocate Phoenix area. Clean driving record. P.O. Box 111, Any Town, 55555.

Special attractions

Watch for special Job Fairs or promotion programs.

TV/Radio —The Phoenix area has a program called "Where the Jobs Are." They often report job openings listed with the Department of Economic Security office and sometimes they promote specific candidates. Speak up for yourself. Contact your local radio station. Contact the talk show host producers. Tell them about your search for work. Ask them if they will give you air time to tell about your skills and the type of work you are looking for. Who knows, they might be willing to start a whole new program.

Housekeepers

If you know that you want to continue doing house cleaning, target your market. Find an area in your town that has homes that are valued at $300,000 or more. Go to the library and find such information as well as information on sales of such homes, on what date and to whom sold. It might be the perfect family to contact. Maybe they just purchased a $500,000 home. Chances are they hire household help. The fact that it is a new move may mean they no longer have access to their prior cleaning service.

What to charge? Find out rates in your area. Call some of the cleaning services. Find out what people are paying. Get yourself bonded. A bond might cost only $50 a year. It will give your future employer peace of mind.

Remember that qualifications are important. Most people are looking to hire housekeepers with references. They want to know you've cleaned homes for others, not just yourself. Caring for your own home doesn't mean you're good, organized, or able to show up on time. If you lack experience, you might want to start working for a cleaning service. You'll gain training and experience.

Be creative

If you love caring for kids, have experience, and have some administrative interests and a convincing manner, create a career. Approach a large employer and offer to establish an in-house child care facility.

Do your homework. Call prepared to discuss your ideas. Know what it takes to implement them. Perhaps the plant has some unused space or a detached building that could be used. Employees could put the space into shape and contribute many of the needed items. Come to your discussion with a list of the requirements for licensing child care facilities in your community. Show how these could be met with your proposed in-plant center.

Another possibility for a new service would be to establish a child-senior care referral service. This might be your own service or established as the service sponsored by a large organization or welfare group.

Sell yourself... go for it!

More Ads

More on responding to ads

Imagine that you are the employer. Take a moment to think again about the other side of the coin. Think about the person who needs help, who calls on an agency or places a help wanted ad in a paper. That person is looking for someone to come into his or her home. It's scary. You feel that you are about to hire a stranger to care for your loved ones or your home. It's a frightening and vulnerable place to be.

As described in the last chapter, write a brief cover letter when you submit your resumé. You are in the position of influencing the tone of your meeting with this person. With the letter, include your resumé and perhaps state your long-term objective. "I'm looking for a job as a nanny..." "I'm looking for a position where I can utilize my housekeeping skills acquired in all the homes I've cleaned." Such objectives will be seen as consistent with the job you are presently seeking.

If you want to do house cleaning, you might want to detail your resumé to state the square footage of each home cleaned. It's one thing to clean or care for a 2,000 sq. ft. home and another if it's 6,000 sq. ft. A future employer will be relieved that you know how to care for a larger home.

If appropriate, you will want to include in your cover letter whether you are willing to work with a family with pets, whether you prefer to live in or out, and even whether you are willing to travel.

Many of the people I placed traveled to places far and near. I had one housekeeper who kept up a 6,000 sq. ft. home in the winters in Arizona and a 10,000 sq. ft. home in England in the summer. I had a nanny who cared for twins on the road. The father was a famous musician. The one thing I cautioned her was not to be influenced by fame. The truth is that traveling and staying in hotels can be cumbersome, especially with twins.

If you are telephoning in response to an ad, have your resumé in front of you. Also have a copy of the NOTES sheet from page 88 in front of you to jot down information. (You may copy or duplicate the NOTES page.) Ask for a job description. When given the chance, detail your past experience as related to the job. Your first words, if true, should indicate the following:

I have

- *Work-related experience*
- *Reliable transportation (Indicate if you live within a 5-mile radius of the job.)*
- *Good, verifiable references*
- *A home phone*
- *Willingness to make a long-term commitment*

DO NOT COMPLAIN ABOUT YOUR PAST OR CURRENT EMPLOYER. Remember, one day this prospective employer will be sitting in that seat. DO NOT COMPLAIN ABOUT YOUR PERSONAL PROBLEMS. Don't ramble on and on. Be a good listener. Ask any further questions about the job. When given the chance, bring up any other matters that should be known early on.

Indicate if you are a non-smoker—a real plus. Most families prefer a non-smoker.

Say if you are allergic to cats or dogs. It can save both of you time and energy if that is acknowledged up front. If you have a fear of dogs, and just cannot work for a family that has a dog, they need to know.

Sometimes when I was screening, I would let that one detail get by me. The applicant and client would meet. It would seem ideal, only to discover that the applicant could not work for a family with dogs. You can't force on a shoe that just doesn't fit. If you do, it won't stay on long. I had one applicant who was greeted by a snake at the door. That's one door I wouldn't enter.

Up front, too, you need to know your role with the family. Many of my clients owned banks, car dealerships, or businesses. Most people treasure their privacy. Most people, even those that want a nanny to be part of the family, still seek time alone with their children. Some families welcome you at their table; some want you at yours. Discuss this while exploring the job. If you want to be part of the family, and they are seeking an employee in the truest sense, then that job is not for you. You would be miserable after a short while.

Interviewing

Can we talk?

From your cover letter, your telephone inquiry, or your visit to an agency, the next step is a personal interview. Cardinal rule number one: Keep the appointment and be punctual. If for some very urgent reason you have to change the appointment, let the agency or the other party know as far in advance as possible. Frankly, my experience has been to doubt the interest of the person. Remember, no one likes to be "stood up," and certainly a prospective employer will start with serious hesitation about your reliability if you don't even make the interview.

If you come to an interview prepared with a resumé, it will impress all concerned.

Hey, good looking...

Good looks is not what this chapter is all about, but cleanliness and a neat appearance are. If you don't take good care of yourself, how can your future employer expect you to take good care of others? This was always a delicate issue for me to handle. I'll never forget one lady who applied for work. She had good references, but I noticed that she was highly underpaid. When she came in to interview in my office, her appearance indicated a need for a bath and a hair cut. So you say you're broke. If you have a few dollars to spare (and I know some of you may not), the beauty school is a good place to start. The better you look, the better you feel. Confidence will emanate. Feeling good, looking good are steps toward getting the job.

If you're Eliza Doolittle, I'm no Professor Higgins. I tried to play ["My Fair Lady"] Higgins once or twice.... I encouraged the candidate to be properly groomed. I emphasized how the client was a stickler for cleanliness and good grooming habits. Unfortunately, the candidate did not realize that she was lacking in that area. I suggested a hair cut (trim) and once again emphasized cleanliness before leaving. The applicant returned to interview with the client, no different than the first time leaving my office. It was a lesson I had to learn. One trip to my office and all the right intentions would not change her grooming habits. So... if you don't practice good grooming, start!

Clothes - Dress for success

The latest fashions are not a concern in this job. Just so you're neat, clean, and professional-looking is all that matters. Wearing a sports shirt instead of a T-shirt will enhance your image; wearing a sweatsuit or cutoffs will detract. But don't get too formal – a baby sitter in a 3-piece suit won't look appropriate for the job.

Attitude - If you've got one, get rid of it

I don't care how good you look and how sweet you smell and how good your resumé looks, if you harbor a chip on your shoulder, it's not your future employer's to bear. Future employers have enough of their own problems. They don't need to add yours to their stack. As a matter of fact, if you beef too much, they may fear that this could be a habit and a price too dear for hiring you. Remember, you are offering them a service... not the other way around. If your attitude is poor, work on it.

Experience can be the best teacher

This is where strong references come into play. However, if you lack experience, stress your stability (providing that's one area you tackled). Point out your past skills and how they can relate to the job you are applying for.

If you worked in a children's clothing department and you are applying for a child care position, mention the amount of time and patience needed to sell clothes for children. Remember back to being the neighborhood sitter. Maybe you helped in the school nursery, or maybe your biggest responsibility meant caring for your younger brother every day after school for four years. Remember that most employers are looking for work-related experience and references.

Education — No one likes a quitter

How important is education to any employer? If you're in high school, complete it. If you dropped out, take your G.E.D. Drop-outs spell one thing to employers ... QUITTERS. Would you want to hire a quitter? This process always stems back to being in the employer's shoes for just one hiring moment. Who would you want to hire, and why? Search yourself for the qualifications you seek in a person to work for you and work toward those qualifications. Take the time to develop a list of qualifications you would seek if you were the one hiring.

Stress your willingness to take CPR and First Aid classes. If you are really serious about getting into the caring industry (industry is such a cold word for such a warm field) consider taking CPR and First Aid training. The truth is, we should all take CPR and First Aid.

Summarize and review the topics covered

Rethink the topics covered. Perhaps it is time to ask the employer to talk about herself or himself. You, too, need to know the personality of the person you will be working with. It may be well to talk a little more about the job description or you may wish to further emphasize your strengths.

Sometimes it's not hard getting the job. Make sure it is what you want and that you see the possibility of a good relationship with the prospective employer.

Ending the interview

Break off the interview gracefully. Perhaps there are other candidates. Perhaps you yourself have other appointments to fill. End the interview with a clear understanding of when a decision will be reached, either on your part of by the employer. If it's a job you want, ask for it.

Follow up. Particularly if you made the approach to a service or a care center, it is courteous to write a short note thanking the interviewer for the opportunity to discuss the work or the opening and indicating that you will hope to hear from them (that is, if you do). Otherwise a simple thank you is courteous and adequate. If you have accepted another position, let them know that as tactfully as possible.

Sample letters covering these possibilities are included in the **SAMPLES** section, page 89.

Household Careers: Nannies, Butler, Maids & More

Firming Up the Agreement

Signed, sealed, delivered

Why contracts? So you will have a firm understanding of the responsibilities on both sides.

Contracts can be useful in that they spell out the job description, hours, days, salaries, and benefits. The contract can be an informal spelling out or a very detailed agreement, pointing out every duty expected. It can state when salary evaluations will occur and what action will cause dismissal.

A sizable institution such as a kindergarten or child care center may have a contract or a set of personnel policies and practices. Perhaps you can ask any prospective employer for "something in writing," but if that person is reluctant or has nothing ready, you will at least have the notes that you took on the suggested NOTES page. A sample contract is also shown in the **Samples** section.

Perhaps the most important understanding is, who is "the employer" and who is "the employee." This may not be as simple as it seems, but it makes a tremendous difference in Social Security, insurance, and tax responsibilities.

Self-employed employee

You will be considered self-employed, or an individual contractor, if you use your own tools and manage your working hours, and direct your own work. Let's say you're a gardener or groundskeeper and you turn up to do the work on your schedule and with your own tools. You are self-employed, and you will file your own Social Security and Medicare payments and report your income as a self-employed person. You will be responsible for your own insurance and for keeping abreast of any changes in requirements or benefits.

If you need more information about self-employed status or clarification of your tax-liability status, call or visit Social Security or ask for a free copy of ***If You're Self-Employed*** (Publication No. 05-10022). You can call a toll-free number 1-800-772-1213 for a booklet about Social Security and a leaflet ***Household Workers***. Though this leaflet is written to the household employer and applies to and spells out the responsibilities of the em-

Firming Up the Agreement

---

ployer, these are your concerns, too. For they tell what tax must be paid (or withheld), what year-end reports are due you, and the like.

Another vitally important leaflet for you, whatever your type of household employment (baby sitter, companion, governess, chauffeur; or any other) is called **How the Fair Labor Standards Act Applies to Domestic Service Workers**. Get a copy from the U.S. Department of Labor, Employment Standards Administration, Wage and Hour Division. WP Publication 1382. Just call the U. S. Department of Labor at (202) 219-8305.

We might note here that other regulations and publications may appear as new administrations take over in Washington, but if you call for these and ask for any others on the topic, you will get what is current.

The issue will arrive as to payroll. You will be considered one of three things: an employee to the person you are working for; an employee to the agency that placed you; or an independent contractor. The first two depend on the arrangement with the agency. Some agencies hire you as their employee. You will negotiate terms of employment with them. They hold the key to your employment and dismissal. Most agencies charge your employer a placement fee. The agency is hired by your employer to locate you, check your references and line up interviews. Upon hire, if your employer pays the agency a placement fee and hires you as his employee, he is the one who can hire or fire you.

The third arrangement is as an independent contractor. Many workers misuse or don't truly understand the meaning behind an independent contractor designation. An independent contractor sets his own hours, buys his own equipment, and generally works for several families. If you run your own cleaning service, you are most likely an independent contractor—if you set the hours and bring your own equipment.

On the other hand, let's say you obtain cleaning work directly or through the recommendation of a friend who puts you in touch directly with a family. You agree to work for them three days a week. They provide the equipment and lay out what you are to do. They are the employer with the obligations already outlined. All you have to do is assure yourself that the obligations are being met and that you are declaring your income at tax time and are paying your employee share of Social Security (unless the employer agrees to pay both his and your share, as many do).

My previous book, **Nannies, Maids & More**, explains all this. Check your library or local bookstore for a copy.

Laws governing the hiring of household help

I am a stickler on this one. As already noted, your employer should be reporting any income paid to you. Your Social Security portion should be deducted and also contributed to by your employer. It is for your best and legal interest to stay honest. What can happen if your income is not reported?

If your income is not reported and your Social Security payment is not deducted (or paid), you will not be able to draw your Social Security benefits when the time comes. That may seem far in the future now, but there are other benefits that may be more immediate. Should you become unable to work, you would not be eligible for Social Security disability if you were not registered in and participating in the Social Security system. Or consider this: You and your spouse want to buy a house but your recorded income is not adequate. What you didn't report won't help you here or in several other situations.

What if I get injured on the job?

This is another reason for knowing precisely who is the employer and under whose and what insurance you are covered. An individual householder will probably carry a Homeowner's Insurance Policy. Will it include liability for an employee injured on the job? If you are employed by a child-care facility or by a hotel or resort, or by any service that is in effect your employer, what insurance do they carry? And, of course, what benefits do they offer?

Inquire of the Insurance Commission in your state about Workmen's Compensation for domestic employees and then find out if your employer contributes to this system. Rules vary by state.

In Arizona, an employer must contribute to the Workmen's Compensation for all domestic employees, excluding companions. The workers themselves may not carry the insurance or contribute to it themselves.

Obviously, if you are self-employed, you will carry your own health and accident insurance. Generally only if the owner of the property where you were working was negligent in some respect about the property and could be shown to have been so, would you be able to look there for any insurance benefits or other award.

All this may seem overly formal and negative, but such agreements and understandings in the beginning may save confusion and unpleasantness later. And these questions alert both you and the employer to possible oversights that can well come back to haunt you later. Remember when neglect cost a Cabinet position?

I Want This Job to Last

For better or worse, richer or poorer

You won't know until you try. But if you outline the type of work you are looking to do and find an employer with your needs, you've made the first step. Remember the precepts in the preceding chapters:

The first thing to do is to try to find a job that meets as many of your qualifications as possible. Be clear about job title, hours, location, salary, and so forth.

If you are looking for a long lasting job, let the future employer or agency personnel know this. If you seek a job with permanency, don't interview for a short term position. If you have a sketchy job history, you are going to have a tougher time proving to a future employer your desire for permanency. Remember, your background will speak for itself.

What determines your length of stay?

Personalities, compatibility — with your employer and other members of the family.

Attitude — of both you and the family that you work for. (If you have a great attitude, but have to deal with family bickering on a daily basis, how long can you digest that?)

Salary — Discuss salaries at the appropriate time of the interview. Determine whether there will be evaluation periods, every six months or whenever. Be clear on all benefits.

Hours/Schedule — Let your future employer know that you are depending on the hours offered. If those alter, it may have you searching for a new job.

Conditions of employment — See attitude above. Lines of responsibility need to be clear. Physical surroundings will also affect your satisfaction with the job.

- **Respect** — Is respect mutually given and received?
- **Discipline** — If you are applying for a child care position, discuss discipline. Make sure you see eye-to-eye on discipline and child-rearing techniques.
- **Praise** — Praise should be a two-way street. Yes, an employer should let you know when you're doing a good job. Likewise, it's always nice for an employer to hear favorable comments also from an employee.
- **Communication** — I found this to be one of the strongest areas of avoidance.

I remember one of my clients with which I had placed a nanny during the first year or so of my business. Three or four years later, her nanny had to leave the job. We soon found her a new nanny. My client called after a week or two and said she was really disappointed in the new nanny.

Number one, it was hard not to compare her to the former nanny. The client's biggest complaint was that the new nanny did not fold clothes. I asked the client one question: "Have you confronted your new nanny? Did you ever ask her to fold the clothes?" The answer on both counts was no. No, she didn't communicate that to the new nanny. The former nanny never needed to be asked. She just did it.

"Well, this new nanny needs a little direction," I said. "Talk to her. If, after your talk, she doesn't fold the clothes, then we'll sit and talk about a replacement. Several weeks later I had a very satisfied client and happy nanny. It just took one little thing... communicating.

On your side, don't be afraid to communicate with your employer. If something comes up and you are going to need unexpected time off, give your employer as much warning as possible. Whoever your employers, treat them the way you would like to be treated if you were in their shoes.

Your own feeling of satisfaction with the job and with your own growth on the job — If you have other goals for the future, this job should be contributing to those goals. This need not be incompatible with a long stay in or satisfaction with the present job.

If you meet all of the above criteria, you may have found the very best situation for you and for your employer.

Quitting

Take this job and...

Before you decide to shove it, give as much thought to leaving the job as you did accepting it. Many people feel that if they just walk off the job because something better awaits them, it doesn't matter how they leave. Wrong!

First off, there's common courtesy. Doing to others as you would like to be treated is one good reason. Another is, you never want to burn a bridge behind you.

You might need those employers for a reference. You might run into them while shopping and you always want to be able to look at a person and feel good about past performance. If the job did not work out, it doesn't mean that somehow that employer might not be able to help with your next or another job in the future.

Before quitting, ask what can be done to salvage an undesirable situation.

If you were made promises and they were broken, talk to your employer. This is where skills in interviewing come into play and also written notes or a contract. If job description and guidelines were strongly communicated, it is less likely that someone will break or misuse those guidelines.

If your job description includes child care and some "light housekeeping," it is best to outline in writing what will be expected of you.

Example: *"Care for a 2-year-old, prepare meals, clean up after all meals, do child's laundry, fold child's clothes, keep child's room neat and tidy."*

With this statement, if your employer starts to add on general ironing and cleaning the bathrooms, you have a better place to negotiate from. If bathrooms are just not your thing, even additional compensation would not get you down on your hands and knees to scrub someone else's toilet. Communicate that during your initial interview.

Quitting

If you were promised a 40-hour work week, and it is reduced to 30 hours, you will need to inform your employer that you need to seek another full-time job, or possibly seek a part-time position, and do they know anyone needing someone 10 hours a week. Remember, even if you don't need these people for a reference now, you never know what the future will hold.

Gaps on resumés do not look good. So you'll want to show how you were employed and by whom. If you left on bad terms, it's hard going back. If you find that the conditions are just too undesirable, give as much notice as possible. Two weeks is generally proper. If emergency situations come up, and they do, that can't be avoided.

Another thing to consider when quitting: If you found the job through an agency and you walk off the job, it looks bad for you and worse for the agency because they placed you with confidence. You might want to use the agency again. So keep all your doors open, do the proper thing, and you will find yourself in a winning situation.

Why jobs end

It isn't always the quality of the work that is at fault if the employer wants to end the job. Four of the top reasons for being fired or dismissed are:

- Poor attitude
- Lateness on the job
- Poor attire
- Lack of communication

And these are all problems in your court.

Keep that in mind as you go into this job market. Mention the positive aspects of the job as you give notice and be sincere in your good wishes for your employers and for their success in finding another employee.

Through the Looking Glass

Creating your own job

Would you like to use your experience to build your own career? Have you enough patience to invest time and experience in order to get established? Can you secure financial backing? If so, there are jobs you can create as an intermediary in any aspect of employment.

At a time in our country when many corporations are downsizing, entrepreneurs are finding ways to make their own businesses flourish. Though there are risks in self-employment, there are many benefits as well, including independence, control, tax benefits, and flexibility.

A little knowledge can be a dangerous thing

This chapter is meant to inspire your imagination, not to be a blueprint for a business plan. The start-up of any enterprise requires a great deal of hard work, including research, research, and more research. As I've mentioned in other chapters, there are legal considerations to explore. You must know how to report income, what taxes you will need to pay and what your Social Security obligations are. You may need to check into licensing and zoning regulations.

There are government and social service agencies and other resources which can help you through the maze of regulations. Read **References** at the back of this book, page 91. Check the library for books on starting a small business. Join a local business association or public service group for valuable contacts and support. Ask friends for the name of a good accountant. The right one will be an invaluable resource. If you can, work for a similar business in order to gain the experience and knowledge to begin your own. Taking the time to prepare yourself beforehand can mean the difference between success and failure in the long run.

Be creative in your business planning and consider these possibilities:

Provide a screening service

Make a list of those advertising for household help. Contact individuals and agencies that hire household help. Offer to screen potential employees. Research FBI reports and offer to check past employment records, non-related character references, and driving records. Check with the Better Business Bureau for ratings of agencies and companies you are screening.

Start a day care center

We have already mentioned the possibility of starting a day care center for employees of large organizations (Chapter 6). *Parenting* magazine annually features a list of employers that cater to the needs of working parents. This is a good contact list.

Start a family home day care

Most parents prefer to have their children at home, but can't afford the luxury. The next best thing is a family home day care center (see definition on page 14). Find out about regulations in your area. Some states require licensing of those caring for more than four non-related children in their home. Even if licensing is not required, get licensed. This will give parents peace of mind.

Many agencies get calls from parents needing family home care. Get yourself on their list. When I first started my agency, I screened family home daycare providers. I contacted the state licensing division and followed their screening procedures. You might consider a screening service for family home day cares. Contact the state and let them know that you are available to screen providers. Place ads for family home day cares both available and needed.

Start a day care center in a major shopping mall

Provide a sitting service for parents who are shopping at the mall. Try to get the mall to support the idea. Charge a parent $2.00 per hour (check rates for your area). Have a center with large glass windows so parents can see their children. Check for licensing requirements.

Provide a child care referral service

Establish a data base of all the child care services in your area and determine a fee for referrals. Such a data base should include pertinent information, such as available days, time, types of care offered, fees, screening procedures, and the like. Include a wide variety of child care, such as sitting services, family home day care, child care for sick children, part-time and full-time nannies. You will provide an invaluable resource for parents and employers.

Offer a senior care referral service

As with the child care referrals, you can research those who can provide senior care and those who are seeking such a service.

Start a family home day care for seniors

Offer an alternative to senior centers and nursing homes. Provide appropriate activities to ease the isolation and boredom that plagues many senior citizens. As with starting home care for children, check local regulations and, if possible, obtain a license.

Start a pet care agency or a pet walking agency

Check with local pet shops, veterinarians, and humane societies for prospects and referrals.

Start a referral service

— for pool cleaning
— for landscaping
— other local domestic help needs

Organize a nanny association in your area

Offer a support group for the nannies in your town. Contact nanny associations in other states and ask if they are willing to share guidelines. Make sure the dues you charge are sufficient to support the organization. Your group should provide: networking, outings, events, speakers, and educational opportunities.

Upgrading your career

More training and specialization may be your key to moving ahead in the future. Try to keep abreast of the demand in your area, or in one in which you would like to work. Watch the number of Help Wanted ads in various fields. Visit a library occasionally and check through professional magazines or business magazines in your field. Enroll in courses offered by local schools or organizations. These things you can do even while working full time.

Keep abreast of advances in the field you're already in. It, too, can continue to be stimulating and increasingly profitable. New opportunities will always be knocking if you're listening.

The Ball Is in Your Court

Take aim...

It is my hope that this book has been a source of ideas, inspiration, and information. Now that you have an informed knowledge of what's out there, it's up to you to apply your own talents and hard work to turn it into what you want it to be.

But don't be frustrated if your dream job doesn't appear right away. Sometimes no matter how hard you try, things may fall through. For example, let me tell you the story behind this book's subtitle.

I had asked Bruce and Jackie Every, who had bought my former household employment agency, to relate any humorous stories about placing household help. I knew from past experience that with the good and the bad comes the funny. After a few days Jackie called back and told me about a family that was looking to hire a nanny. They literally told Jackie, "If the dog likes the nanny, she's hired."

What more can I say. No matter how hard one tries to follow the guidelines in seeking household employment, sometimes it all comes down to... "*If the dog likes you, you're hired!*"

I'd love to hear about *your* experiences. Please write to me c/o Five Star Publications, P.O. Box 3142, Scottsdale, AZ 85271-3142.

— *Linda F. Radke*

LAND-A-JOB

THE EMPLOYMENT GAME

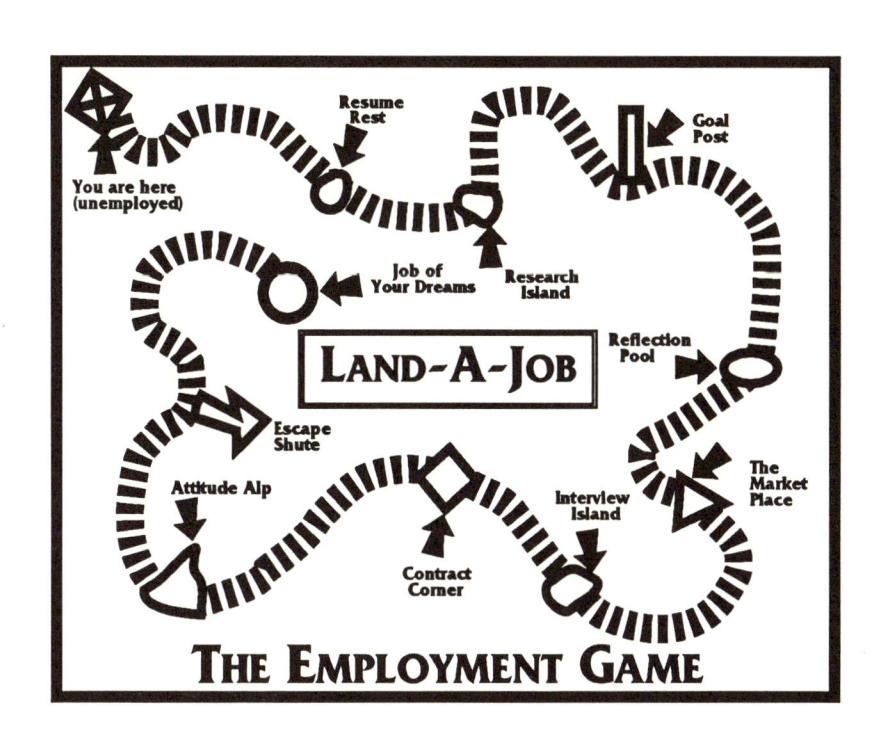

- You are here (unemployed)
- Resume Rest
- Goal Post
- Job of Your Dreams
- Research Island
- Reflection Pool
- Escape Shute
- Attitude Alp
- Contract Corner
- Interview Island
- The Market Place

GET OUT OF UNEMPLOYMENT!

Free Chance

Play the Employment Game!

Household Careers: Nannies, Butler, Maids & More

Samples

It's right here in black and white...

The following pages contain sample forms. They may be duplicated for your own use.

Household Careers: Nannies, Butler, Maids & More

RESUMÉ OUTLINE

Name _____
Social Security # _____
Address _____
City _____ **Zip Code** _____
Phone (day) _____ (eve.) _____

Job Title
   (position or positions sought)

Experience
   (type of work and number of years employed)

Education

Special Training or Courses
   Red Cross (or other) First Aid Course
   CPR training

Facilities Offered   (for those giving care in own homes)
   Approved by..... (indicate licenses or government agencies)
   Possibly include picture of facility or home

Personal Information
   Marital status
   Children?

References
   Include both professional and personal references
   Include full names and telephone numbers

Samples

SAMPLE RESUMÉ

James R. James Tel: (000) 123-9876
123 West 2nd Street
Anytown, AA 12301 Soc. Sec.#: 102-08-0001

Position Sought: Elder companion

Objective: To serve as companion or respite caregiver to one or more elder persons from mid-morning to approximately 5 p.m. weekdays

Career Objective: Position in geriatric health care field or obtain an LPN degree. Am currently working toward a degree in night classes at Anytown Community College.

Education: 1992 graduate Anytown Central High School.

Experience: 1989 - 1992 After-school and summer employment at Roberts Adult Day Care Center West, 7th Street, Anytown

Began helping with yard work, then inside work putting away equipment and the like, 1991-92 began doing individual errands for the day care patrons.

For two of the patrons have helped out at home on one or two weekends a month. (See references.)

Special Training:

Red Cross First Aid Course

CPR course through Anytown Fire Department
(show expiration date if appropriate)

Driver Education in high school

Have attended rehabilitation seminars at the Adult Day Care Center.

Personal Information: Have clean driver's record; have driver's license and chauffeur's license. Parents keep up car insurance.

References:

Dr. R. J. Roberts, Director Sidney Ash, Principal
Roberts Adult Day Care Center Anytown High School
West Seventh Street Tel: (000) 245-5432
Anytown, AA, 12301
Tel: (000) 705-2121 Mrs. Jane Smith
  (daughter of J.C. Smith)
Rev. Lester Jones 500 First Street
Anytown Methodist Church Anytown, AA 12301
200 First Street Anytown, AA, 12301 Tel: (000) 245- 2101, home
Tel: (000) 705-8234 705-1300, work

Household Careers: Nannies, Butler, Maids & More

SAMPLE RESUMÉ

Sarah M. Jones Tel: (000) 987-6543
800 East 5th Street Apt. 101
Milltown, AA 10101 Soc. Sec. No. 111-01-0041

Position Sought Housecleaning
Daily work – live out – in private home

Experience 1990 to present
Madison Hotel Resort
Grant Road, Milltown
Room attendant
Supervisor: Vera Butler   Tel: (000) 234-3400

June 1988-1990
Ultra Mill Offices, Milltown
Maintenance staff
Jennie Black, Supervisor Tel: (000) 234-8000

June 1984 - June 1988
Big Burger, Milltown Grant Road
Waitress

June 1980-1984
Variety Store, Valley Heights, AB
Salesperson
Left to move to Milltown

Education GED

References Supervisors listed above

Ms. Amy Cox, Postmistress
Milltown , AA   10101
Tel: (000) 234-5000

James Edwards
Milltown Bowling Club
P.O. Box 10
Milltown, AA 10101
Tel: 234-5234 (evenings)

Samples

COVER LETTERS FOR RESUMÉS

In reply to an ad in a Help Wanted Column with Box Number given:

Dear Holder of Box 00:

In reply to your ad in the Domestic Services column of the Anytown Gazette, Sunday, May 6, I am enclosing my resumé as requested. I look forward to hearing from you and to further details about the position. You may reach me at the telephone number or address on the resumé.

Sincerely,

To an unknown person in an organization that has not advertised:

(Call and ask for the name of a person to whom to address the letter.)

COVER LETTERS FOR RESUMÉS

To head of a Human Resources Department at a motel or hotel:

Dear   :

 I am interested in joining the housekeeping staff of the Regal Resort. My resumé is enclosed. As you will see, I have experience in a related field and a good work record. I admire the Regal Resort and would be pleased to be on its staff. May I call for a personal interview? If you prefer to contact me, I can be reached at the address or telephone number on the resumé in early morning or most evenings.

Respectfully,

Samples

COVER LETTERS FOR RESUMÉS

To the head of a child care center:

(Call and ask for the name of the director if you do not know it.)

Ms. M. Jones, Director
Happy Child Day Care Center
Anytown

Dear Ms. Jones:

Is there an opening on the staff of the Happy Child Day Care Center? I have recently moved into your area and wish to continue my child care career here. As you will see from the enclosed resumé, I have had both training and experience in day care work. I wish to continue in this field. While I seek full-time work, my hours are flexible. I'll call in a few days for a personal interview.

Sincerely,

Household Careers: Nannies, Butler, Maids & More

APPLICATION FOR EMPLOYMENT

APPLICATION FOR HOUSEHOLD EMPLOYMENT

We are an equal opportunity employer, dedicated to a policy of non-discrimination in hiring on any basis, including race, creed, color, age, sex, religion or national origin.

PERSONAL INFORMATION   PLEASE PRINT!   DATE _____

Full Name _____ Social Security Number _____

Address _____ How Long? _____

Previous Address _____ How Long? _____

Phone Number: Home _____ Work _____ Message _____

Are you a U.S. citizen? _____ If no, are you eligible to be employed under a visa permit? _____

State age if under 18 or over 70 : _____ Marital Status _____ Number & ages of dependents: _____

Are you a smoker? _____ Swimmer? _____ Are you certified in: ☐ CPR   ☐ First Aid   ☐ Life Saving

Is your certification current? _____ Date of expiration: _____

Transportation Available: _____ Do you have a chauffeur's license? _____

Have you ever been bonded? _____ If yes, what job(s)? _____

Have you ever been denied bond coverage? _____ If yes, please explain: _____

Have you ever entered a plea of guilty or been convicted of any crime or any moving traffic violations? _____

If yes, please explain: _____

How long have you lived in this state? _____ How did you hear about this job? _____

Please list other position(s) you are applying for: 1. _____

2. _____   3. _____

If you are applying for child care, what age(s) do you prefer to work with? _____

Will you work for a family with pets? _____

Please check your availability (check all that apply)   Full-time ☐   Part-time ☐   (list hours) _____

Live-in ☐   Live-out ☐   Temporary assignments ☐   Relocate out-of-state ☐

Other _____ Rate of pay expected: _____

EDUCATIONAL BACKGROUND

	Circle last year completed	Year graduated	Name and location of school
Elementary School	5 6 7 8	_____	_____
High School	1 2 3 4	_____	_____
College	1 2 3 4	_____	_____
Vocational School	1 2 ____ mos.	_____	_____

Foreign languages you speak, read or write well: _____

PHYSICAL RECORD

Do you have any conditions which might limit your ability to perform the job applied for? _____

If yes, please explain _____

DRIVER'S LICENSE

Do you possess a valid driver's license? _____ If yes, state issued _____ D.L. # _____

Name as it appears on the license _____ Expiration date _____

How far do you live from this job site?   ☐ less than a mile   ☐ 1-2 miles   ☐ 2-4 miles   ☐ 5 miles
                                          ☐ 6-10 miles   ☐ 10 miles or more

Samples

EMPLOYMENT HISTORY
List below all past employment, beginning with the most recent. Use separate sheet of paper if necessary.

Name of employer _____ Supervisor's name _____
Address _____ City, State, Zip _____
Phone number: Home _____ Office _____
Employed from _____ to _____ If child care, number of children and ages _____
If housecleaning, number of square feet _____ Days and hours worked _____
Job description _____
Reason for leaving _____ Ending salary _____

Name of employer _____ Supervisor's name _____
Address _____ City, State, Zip _____
Phone number: Home _____ Office _____
Employed from _____ to _____ If child care, number of children and ages _____
If housecleaning, number of square feet _____ Days and hours worked _____
Job description _____
Reason for leaving _____ Ending salary _____

Name of employer _____ Supervisor's name _____
Address _____ City, State, Zip _____
Phone number: Home _____ Office _____
Employed from _____ to _____ If child care, number of children and ages _____
If housecleaning, number of square feet _____ Days and hours worked _____
Job description _____
Reason for leaving _____ Ending salary _____

May we contact the employers listed above? _____ If not, which one(s) do you not wish us to contact? _____

CHARACTER REFERENCES
List below the names of two people not related to you, whom you have known at least one year:

Name & Address   Name & Address
_____   _____
_____   _____
_____   _____

Phone _____ Years known _____   Phone _____ Years known _____

The facts in my application are true and complete. You are hereby authroized to make any investigations of my personal history and financial and credit status through any credit agencies of your choice. I understand that any misrepresentation or omission of facts is cause for termination of employment. Further, I understand and agree that any employment gained is for no definite period of time and may, regardless of the date of payment of my wages and salary, be terminated at any time without any previous notice.

Signature _____ Date _____

IN ORDER TO PROCESS YOUR APPLICATION, ALL INFORMATION MUST BE COMPLETE!

© 1989 Five Star Publications

SAMPLES – May be duplicated.

RECORD KEEPING:
for noting each job application

NOTES

Response to ad in _____

Date _____ Appointment time _____ Place _____

Contact name _____

Position _____

General duties _____

Begin   _____

Pay   _____

Hours   _____

Insurance? _____

Income tax withheld? _____

Social Security to be collected? _____

Other information _____

    Children _____

    Vacation time _____

Agreement on next contacts _____

THANK YOU LETTERS FOR INTERVIEWS

To follow up an interview. Address to the person with whom you talked.

Dear   :

Thank you for discussing the position of _____ with me. I appreciate the time and care you took in explaining your needs to me. I am interested in the position and look forward to hearing your decision. I Hope it is a "yes," but even if not, I wish you continued success.

Sincerely,

To follow up an interview and inform the interviewer of your decision:

Thank you for discussing the position of _____ with me. Certainly it is in the field of my interest, however, the interview that was still pending when I saw you has resulted in a firm offer, which I am accepting. Thank you again for your consideration.

Sincerely,

Household Careers: Nannies, Butler, Maids & More

SAMPLES – May be duplicated.　　　　　Contract Form

EMPLOYMENT AGREEMENT

City _____

Date_____

Between: Employer _____

Address _____

Employee _____

Address _____

Position _____

which may include the following duties:

_____

_____

Days to be worked _____

Hours _____

Vacation (or leave time)_____

Salary rate_____ to be paid _____

review_____

Benefits _____ Social Security 　_____ Health insurance

_____ Meals 　　　　　_____ Transportation

_____ Workmen's compensation

Other _____

The employee undertakes to provide the following:

_____ CPR certificate 　_____ Current TB test result

_____ Dept. of Motor Vehicle Report

Other _____

Ending of this agreement may be by either party with 2 weeks' notice or for unsatisfactory performance by either party.

References will be provided by employer on request.

Signed _____ Employer

_____ Employee

References

Useful Addresses

National Association of Nannies
1681 S. Dayton St.
Denver, CO 80231

Private training school for nannies

International Nanny Association
P.O. Box 26522
Austin, TX 78755

Has free publication *"So You Want To Be A Nanny."* Also ***Directory of Nanny Training Programs, Nanny Placement Agencies and Special Services***, *for which there is a charge.*

Council for Early Childhood Professional Recognition
1718 Connecticut Ave., NW Suite 500
Washington, DC 20009

National Academy of Nannies, Inc.
3300 E. 1st Ave. Suite 520
Denver, CO 90206

American Council of Nanny Schools
c/o Joy Shelton
Delta College
University Center, MI 48710

Has a list of nanny schools and agencies.

National Executive Housekeepers Association
1001 Eastwind Drive, Suite 301
Westerville, OH 43081

Senior Companion Project *(Volunteerism)*
Washington Urban League
2900 Newton Street, N.E.
Washington, DC 20018

National Domestic Workers Union *(Hospitality Industries)*
42 Spring Street, S.W., Suite 246
Atlanta, GA 30303

Offers senior citizen and employment services. Sponsors Maid Honor Day annually.

Services Employees International Union
1313 L Street, N.W.
Washington, DC 20005

Ivor Spencer International School for Butler Administrators/Personal Assistants
12 Little Bornes, Alleyn Park, Dulwich, London
SE21 8SE, England
Fax 081-670 0055

References

Publications

General

Dictionary of Occupational Titles
Rev. 4th Edition. Vol 1.
U. S. Department of Labor 1991

Occupations are named and described in various categories, such as "Service Occupations." Descriptions of the jobs are overwhelming in their detail and inclusiveness. Still, the book is a valuable reference and is available in most libraries.

Occupational Outlook Handbook
Bulletin 2400 May 1992
U.S. Department of Labor
Bureau of Labor Statistics

May be seen in a library or ordered from the Superintendent of Documents.

Very readable and useful descriptions of work in various areas, such as "Preschool Workers" or "Private Household Workers," for example. Describes and comments on the field, describes working conditions, qualifications needed and advancement in the area, earnings, job outlook, and related occupations.

Vocational Careers Sourcebook
Kathleen M. Savage and Karen Hill, Editors
Gale Research, Inc. 1992

A superb new compilation of sources for evaluating 135 vocational occupations. Lists job descriptions, career guides, Associations and certification agencies, test guides, information sources, as well as general summary of each field and its outlook, Look for it in libraries.

Nannies, Maids & More
Linda F. Radke 1989
Five Star Publications

A Complete Guide for Hiring Household Help. Valuable for its information about what employers are seeking and where they look as well as discussion of employers' obligations to employees and expectations of those they hire.

Places Rated Almanac
Richard Boyer and David Savageau
Prentice-Hall Travel 1989
New York: A Division of Simon and Schuster

An excellent source of information about locales all over the country. Covers such items as jobs, cost of living, recreation, climate, the arts.

Exploring Careers
Revised 1990-1991 Edition
Based on U.S. Dept. of Labor Statistics
JIST Works, Inc.

Encyclopedia of Careers and Vocational Guidance
Vol. 3 General and Special Careers
8th Edition 1990
William E. Hopke, Editor-in-chief
Chicago: J. G. Ferguson Co.

Includes some household careers. Gives definitions, nature of work, requirements, employment outlook, and earnings.

Exploring Careers in Child Care
Jean Ipsa
Revised edition, 1988
New York: Rosen Publications Group, Inc.

Covers the whole range of careers and professions related to child care. Gives names and addresses of organizations related to child care and child care professions.

Books on Preparing Resumés

Most libraries will have quite a collection of books on this subject. Here are a few that may be particularly useful.

How to Write Better Resumés, Third Edition.
Adele Lewis
Barron's Educational Series   1989

Gives many examples.

The Perfect Resumé
Revised and updated.
Tom Jackson
Doubleday   1990

Discusses career outlooks for the '90s, and the purposes of a resumé and how to achieve these purposes whatever your job interest. Contains work sheets and samples.

Power Resumés
Ron Tepper
John Wiley & Sons 1989

Goes beyond resumé writing to whole job search topic. Very comprehensive and detailed.

The Resumé Guide for Women of the '90s
Kim Marino
Tangerine Press 1990

Includes housewives and moms entering or reentering the job market.

Many suggestions directed to first-time job seekers. Includes scenarios of women and then a sample of the resumé for each.

American Salaries and Wages Survey
Arsen J. Darnay
Gale Research Inc. 1991

Shows high and low salaries for jobs by categories in many cities across the country. Figures in this edition are 1990 figures.

Housekeeping

Useful books for updating techniques and teaching newer, more efficient techniques and products and equipment.

Household Hints and Handy Tips
Reader's Digest Editors
New York: Reader's Digest Association, Inc.
1988 $36.95
Distributed by Random House

Speed Cleaning
Jeff Campbell and The Clean Team
Second Edition
A Dell Trade Paperback
New York: Dell Publishing (A Division of Bantam Doubleday Dell, Publishing Group, Inc.)
1991 $5.99

Mary Ellen's Clean House
Mary Ellen Pinkham with Dale Burg
Crown Publishing Group
1993 $20.00

Index

A

Advertising 38, 39, 41
   responding to 45
   by telephone 46
Attendant, room 16

B

Baby sitter 14
Business opportunities 70
Butler 8, 16
   opportunities 7
   salaries 8
   school for 8
   training 8
Butler administrator 9
Butler bodyguard 8, 9

C

Career counseling 26
Caretaker 17
Caterer 18
Chauffeur 17
Child care 14, 43
   considerations for choosing 24
   creating own job in 43
   expanding field 12
   for large employer 43
   jobs in 14
Child care referral service 72
Classifications, job 56–58
Community job listing services 38

Community job services 38, 42
Companion 15
   elder care 15
Contractor, independent 58
Contracts 55
   ingredients 55
   value of 55
Cook 17
Couples 18
Couples, live-in, live-out 18
Cover letter
   examples of 30
   purpose of 30
   what to include 46
Creating own job 43, 69

D

Day care center
   in a shopping mall 72
   starting your own 71
Day care provider
   family, home 14
Definitions
   of household careers 6, 13, 13–19
Demand
   how to analyze 34
Department of Labor, U.S. 57
Dictionary of Occupational Titles 19
Dismissal, reasons for 67
Dissatisfaction with job 65–67

Domestic Screening Kit, The 2
Driver 17

E

Elder care
  companion 15
  respite care 15
Employee 56
Employee or employer
  distinction between 56
  sources of information 56
Employers
  potential 35
  ways to reach 35
Employment agencies
  advantages of using 35, 36
  information needed for 36
  preparation for using 36
  researching 36

F

Family home day care
  for children 71
  for seniors 72
  starting your own 71

G

Gardener 17
Governess 14

H

Homeowner's insurance 59
House worker 16
Household Workers 56

Household workers
  demand for 11
Housekeeper 15
  exploring market for 43
  requirements for 43
Housekeeper, head 15
How the Fair Labor Standards Act Applies to Domestic Service Workers 57

I

If You're Self-Employed 56
Independent contractor 58
Injuries, job related 59
Insurance 59–60
Interview, personal
  follow up 53
  managing 49, 52
  obtaining information in 53
  preparation for 50–51
Ivor Spencer 7
Ivor Spencer International
  School for Butlers 7

J

Job classifications 56, 56–58
Job dissatisfaction 65–67
Job duration
  requirements for 62
Job fairs 42
Job loss 67
Job opportunities
  how to find 38
  special sources 42
Job programs 42
Job related injuries 59

L

Launderer 17
Laws on household help 58
   importance of observing 60
Likes and dislikes 26

M

Maid 16
Market research 34
Marketing yourself 33
   essentials 34
   targeting prospects 43
Mother's helper 14
   example 24

N

Nannies 14
   demand for 12
   options in jobs
   salaries 22, 25
Nannies, Maids & More 2, 58
Nanny association
   organizing 73
Newspaper advertising 38

O

Occupational Careers Sourcebook 19
Occupational Outlook Handbook, The 19
Opportunities (see Job opportunities)
Options: A Directory of Child and Senior Services 3

P

Party server 18
Pay
   comparative rates 20-22
   chart 22
Pet care agency 73
Preschool worker 15
Prospects
   how to target 43

Q

Quitting a job 65

R

References 29
   as first contact 33
   importance of
   in resumés 29
Referral service
   as a job possibility 44
   starting your own 73
Resources 70, 73
Resumés
   characteristics of 28–31
   organizing facts for 28
   preparing, sources of help in 28
   tailoring to fit 45
Room attendant 16

S

Salaries
   comparative 22
   in child care 25

Salvaging a job 66
Screening service 70
Self-analysis
 of job interests 23
Self-employed 56
 considerations 70
Senior care referral service 72
Server, party 18
Sitters 18
 baby 14
 for elderly 18
 for pets 18
 house 18
Social Security 58

T

Teacher's aide 25
Temporary positions 26
The Domestic Screening Kit 2
TV/Radio
 job programs 42

U

Upgrading your career 73

W

Workmen's Compensation 59

Y

Yard worker 17
Yellow Pages
 as job source listing 39

Other Five ★ Star ★ Publications

SHAKESPEARE FOR CHILDREN: The Story of Romeo and Juliet. Nominated for the 1990 Benjamin Franklin Children's Storybook Award. Recommended for 4th grade and up.
ISBN 0-9619853-3-X. $9.95

THE SIXTY-MINUTE SHAKESPEARE: Romeo and Juliet. A one-hour acting edition that includes affordable set design, sound and prop requirements, costume suggestions, definition of unfamiliar terms and complete and easy-to-follow stage directions. Recommended for 7th grade and up. ISBN 0-9619853-8-0 $3.95

Sound effects tape available $5.00

SHAKESPEARE: To Teach or Not To Teach. This approach makes it easy for any teacher to inspire students with the works of William Shakespeare. The clear and simply laid out text explores the beauty and genius of the world's greatest dramatist. Written for grades 3 and up.
ISBN 1-877749-03-6. $19.95

NANNIES, MAIDS & MORE: The Complete Guide for Hiring Household Help. Discusses all angles of hiring help on your own, and using employment agencies. If you find yourself hiring more than two different workers a year, this reading is a must. Author owned a household employment agency for nearly five years; helped over 1,000 families secure help and screened more than 5,000 candidates.
ISBN 0-9619853-2-1 $14.95

OPTIONS: An Arizona Directory of Child & Senior Services. 1987 & 1989. An Arizona statewide directory listing services specializing in child or senior care. The 1989-90 edition features a national
listing of nanny schools and agencies. $9.95

THE DOMESTIC SCREENING KIT. 1985. Do-it-yourself kit for hiring any type of household help. Contains all the forms necessary for screening, interviewing, and hiring household staff. Won national attention. $24.95

Check with your local bookstore first for availability of any of these publications. If you cannot locate them, write to: **Five Star Publications**, P.O. Box 3142, Scottsdale, AZ 85271-3142 or call: (602) 941-0770 (in Arizona) or toll free, 1-800-545-STAR, ext. 14. Prices subject to change.

NOTES

NOTES

NOTES